Our Colorful Multilingual Adventures

Hi Everybody!!!
My name is Rosie and I am the author of this colorful Study Guide that I have created just for you!!!
Swahili is a beautiful language spoken in Africa and all over the world. My mission is to help introduce you to the basics of Swahili that will get you started on your journey to becoming Multilingual.
Thank you so much for your love and support!!
Visit our Youtube Channel
Multilingual Stars Academy and start learning different languages with me and my family today!!!!

5 Fun Facts!!

1. Swahili is predominantly a mix of local Bantu languages and Arabic.
2. Swahili is the national language in Tanzania, Kenya, Rwanda, Uganda, African Union, Democratic Republic of Congo.
3. Swahili is one of the most widely spoken languages in Africa with more than 140 million speakers.
4. The Kanga is a popular swahili garment.
5. There are about 15 main Swahili dialects, as well as several pidgin forms in use.

HuJambo

(who-Jahm-bow)

How are you?

Sijambo

(see-Jahm-bow)

I am fine.

Rafiki/Friend

(rah-fee-key)

uhuru

(uu-who-roo)

Freedom

Nikiongozi wa leo.

(knee-key-ohn-go-Zee wah leh-oh)

Today I am a Leader.

Jua/Sun

(jew-ahh)

Nakupenda
(Nah-coo-pen-dah)
I Love You

Karibuni
(kah-ree-boo-knee)

Welcome All

Habari /Shikamoo Hello

(hah-bah-ree) / (she-kah-moh)

Kwaheri

(kwah-heh-ree)

Good-bye

Tuonane tena

(2-oh-nah-neh teh-nah)

See you soon

Ninafuraha kukutana na wewe

(knee-nah-foo-rah-hah cou-cou-tah-nah nah weh-weh)

Nice to meet you

Months
Miezi

Januari	(jahn-u-ah-ree)
Februari	(fehb-rue-ah-ree)
Machi	(mah-chee)
Aprili	(ah-pree-lee)
Mei	(meh-e)
Juni	(jew-knee)
Julai	(jew-lah-e)
Agosti	(ah-go-ss-t)
Septemba	(sehp-tehm-bah)
Oktoba	(ohk-toh-bah)
Novemba	(no-vehm-bah)
Desemba	(d-sehm-bah)

Siku Za Wiki

(see-coo) (zah) (we-key)

Days of The Week

Jumapili **Sunday**

(jew-mah-p-lee)

Jumatatu **Monday**

(jew-mah-tah-2)

Jumanne **Tuesday**

(jew-mah-nay)

Jumatano **Wednesday**

(jew-mah-tah-no)

Alhamisi **Thursday**

(ahl-hah-me-c)

Ijumaa **Friday**

(e-jew-mah)

Jumamosi **Saturday**

(jew-mah-moh-c)

Nambari

(nahm-bah-ree)

Numbers

(sue-fue-ree)	**sufuri**	0
(moh-jah)	**moja**	1
(mm-b-lee)	**mbili**	2
(tah-2)	**tatu**	3
(nn-nay)	**nne**	4
(tah-no)	**tano**	5
(c-tah)	**sita**	6
(sah-bah)	**saba**	7
(nah-nay)	**nane**	8
(t-sah)	**tisa**	9
(coo-me)	**kumi**	10

Rangi Colors

(rahn-gee)

Nyeusi Black

(knee-you-c)

Zambarau Purple

(zahm-bah-rah-ou)

Machungwa Orange

(mah-choon-gwah)

Nyekundu Red

(knee-yuh-coon-do)

Manjano Yellow

(mahn-jah-no)

Buluu Blue

(boo-lou)

Kijani Green

(key-jah-knee)

Jamaa/Family

(jah-mah)

Mama Mother

(mah-mah)

Baba Daddy

(bah-bah)

dada Sister

(dah-dah)

kaka Brother

(kah-kah)

babu grandfather

(bah-boo)

nyanya grandmother

(nyah-nyah)

Daily Affirmations

Mimi ni mrembo

(me me knee mm-rehm-bow)

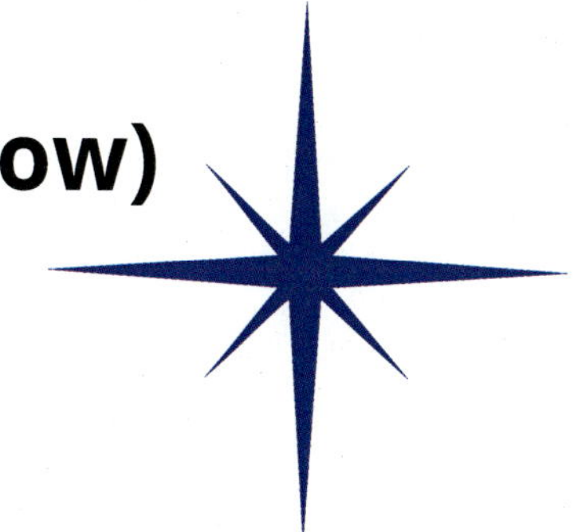

I am Beautiful

Mimi ni mzuri

(me me knee mm-zoo-ree)

I am good/fine

Mimi ninatosha

(me me knee-nah-toh-shah)

I am Enough

Hakuna Matata

(ha-coo-nah mah-tah-tah)

No Worries

Safari/Journey

(sah-fah-ree)

Simba

(Sim-bah)

Lion

Matunda

(mah-toon-dah)

Fruit

nanasi

(nah-nah-c)

Pineapple

tufaha

(2-fah-hah)

Apple

tikiti maji

(t-key-t mah-g)

Watermelon

Zabibu

(zah-b-boo)

Grapes

Chungwa

(choon-gwah)

Orange

Ndizi

(nn-d-z)

Banana

Pea Pear

(peh-ah)

Kwanzaa

(kwahn-zah)

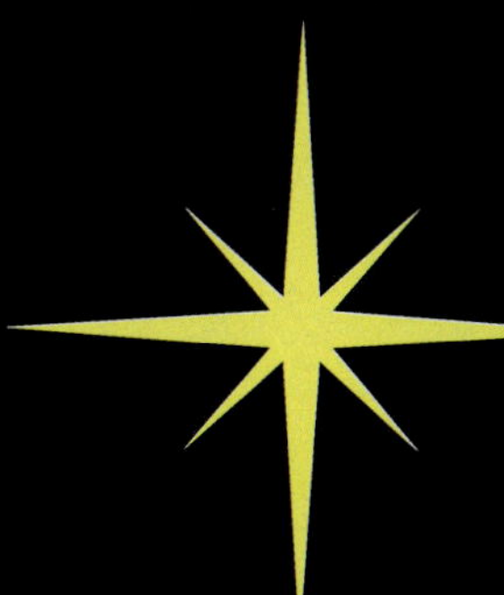

Nguzo Saba

(nn-guu-zoh sah-bah)

Seven principles

Umoja = Unity

(oo-moh-jah)

Kujichagulia = Self-Determination

(koo-g-cha-goo-lee-yah)

Ujima = Collective Work and Responsibility

(oo-g-mah)

Ujamaa = Cooperative Economics

(oo-jah-mah)

Nia = Purpose

(nee-AH)

Kuumba = Creativity

(koo-OOM-bah)

Imani = Faith

(ee-MAH-knee)

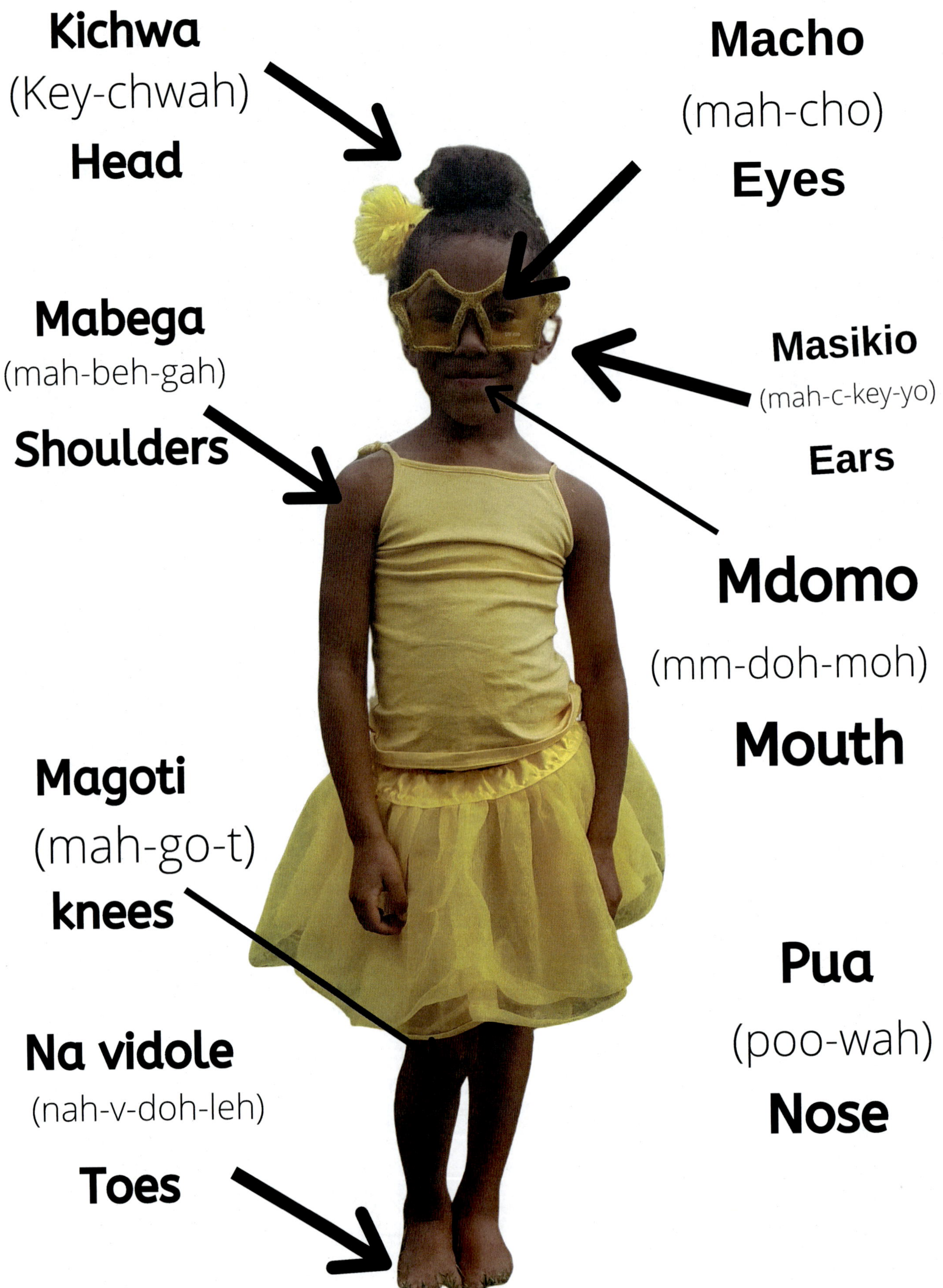
Kichwa
(Key-chwah)
Head
Macho
(mah-cho)
Eyes
Mabega
(mah-beh-gah)
Shoulders
Masikio
(mah-c-key-yo)
Ears
Mdomo
(mm-doh-moh)
Mouth
Magoti
(mah-go-t)
knees
Pua
(poo-wah)
Nose
Na vidole
(nah-v-doh-leh)
Toes

Habari Za Asubuhi

(ha-bah-ree zah ah-sue-boo-he)

Good Morning

Habari za Mchana

(ha-bah-ree zah mm-cha-nah)

Good Afternoon

Habari za jioni

(ha-bah-ree zah g-oh-knee)

Good evening

Alfabeti

Alphabet

A (ah) B (beh) CH (cheh) D (deh) E (eh) F (ef)

G (geh) H (heh) I (ee)

J (jeh) K (kah) L (Leh) M (em) N (en) O (oh) P (peh)

R (err reh) S (seh)

T (teh) U (oo) sounds like (oops) V (veh) W (weh) Y (yeh) Z (zeh)

Asante Sana

(ah-sahn-teh Sah-nah)

Thank you very much!!

About the Authors

Shylene Santiago and her children, founders of Learn A Language 4 Fun,LLC have dedicated over 4 years to creating songs, educational YouTube videos and designing study guides to introduce students to the basics of over 10 different languages.

After extensive research and speaking to many educators and parents, Santiago finally came to understand that because of low funding in the educational system, language programs are often not offered in under privileged communities. And realizing the need of representation for more Black multilingual teachers, Shylene decided to utilize her passion and language skills to create a business that can be a resource our communities can depend on.

Inquiries should be addressed to shylene_santiago@yahoo.com

www.learnalanguageforfun.com

Made in the USA
Columbia, SC
06 August 2022